# INSPIRATIONAL LIVES

# SIMON COWELL
## GLOBAL MUSIC MOGUL

**Debbie Foy**

WAYLAND

First published in 2010 by Wayland

Copyright © Wayland 2010

Wayland
338 Euston Road
London NW1 3BH

Wayland Australia
Level 17/207 Kent Street
Sydney, NSW 2000

Senior editor: Camilla Lloyd
Designer: Rob Walster
Picture researcher: Shelley Noronha

Picture acknowledgments: The author and publisher would like to thank the following for allowing their pictures to be reproduced in this publication: Cover: © Getty Images; © Hulton-Deutsch Collection/CORBIS: 6; © Bettman/ CORBIS: 9; © Getty Images: 4, 16, 18, 26, 27; © AFP/Getty Images; Courtesy of Dover College: 8; Â©Lee Roth/ STARMAX/allaction.co.u /Starmax/ EMPICS Entertainment: 7; © Starshock/ Photoshot: 13; © Everett/Photoshot: 21; © UPPA/Photoshot: 24; © Fremantle Media Ltd/Rex Features: 5; © Richard George/ Rex Features: 11; © Rex Features: 12; © Skyline Features/Rex Features: 14; © ITV/Rex Features: 15; © Fremantle Media Ltd/Rex Features: 19; © Stewart Cook/ Rex Features: 28; © Richard Young/Rex Features: 29; Talkback Thames/Syco: 17, 20, 22, 23, 25.

British Library Cataloguing in Publication Data:
Foy, Debbie.
Simon Cowell.- (Inspirational lives)
1. Cowell, Simon, 1959- 2. Television personalities-Great Britain-Biography-Juvenile literature.
3. Sound recording executives and producers-Great Britain- Biography- Juvenile literature.
I. Title II. Series
791.4'5'092-dc22

ISBN: 978 0 7502 6272 9

Printed in China

Wayland is a division of Hachette Children's Books, an Hachette UK company.

www.hachette.co.uk

# Contents

# The birth of TV's Mr Nasty

When Mr Cowell first hit our screens in 2001 for the first series of *Pop Idol*, he was not so much famous as **infamous**. He was the man we all loved to hate – TV's Mr Nasty.

Before he found fame, Simon Cowell was a behind-the-scenes **music executive** who had known some success managing bands and singers, but was yet to set the UK music scene alight. *Pop Idol* was to change all that.

## HONOURS BOARD

**Here are some of Simon's most famous put-downs:**

*"When you sing, you remind me of a cod on a fishmonger's slab."*

*"I don't think you know how bad you sound, no seriously."*

*"You sing like Mickey Mouse on helium."*

*On the brink of UK television domination, Simon Cowell had a lot to smile about!*

At the early *Pop Idol* auditions, Simon complained that the judges' feedback to the contestants sounded false and overly polite. The most direct and honest comments were from Simon, who delivered withering put-downs such as, "I'm afraid to say that really hurt my ears." His criticism of the contestants' songs, voices, clothing and even looks soon earned him a reputation in the media of being the villain of the show.

Fame came late and very suddenly for Simon. At 42 he was unknown, at 43 he was famous in the UK, but only a few years later he was famous all over the world. Series 1 of *Pop Idol* changed the music industry forever, but it also launched Simon Cowell on his incredible journey to being one of the most powerful music **moguls** the world has ever seen.

# INSPIRATION

Simon knew that Ant and Dec were part of the success of the programme. Their **deadpan** humour was a great **antidote** to the show's tension. Ant and Dec helped the series become a huge success and Simon become famous.

Ant and Dec established a joke about Simon and his high-waisted trousers that would haunt him for years!

# The early days

Simon's first victim was his mum. It was Christmas Day and Julie Cowell walked down the stairs, all dressed up for lunch and proudly wearing a new white fur hat. "Mum, you look like a poodle," Simon announced. He was four years old!

Simon Phillip Cowell was born on 7 October 1959 in Brighton. He grew up in Elstree, Hertfordshire, with his younger brother, Nicholas, his three half-brothers, Tony, John and Michael and half-sister, June.

His father, Eric, was an estate agent and his mother, Julie, an ex-ballet dancer. Simon had a happy childhood, in a large, comfortable house called Abbots Mead with plenty of rooms for playing hide-and-seek and enormous gardens to roam in. The family employed a gardener, a housekeeper and a live-in nanny to look after the three youngest children – Tony, Simon and Nicholas.

## WOW!

Simon was a practical joker and one day swapped the handkerchief in his father's suit pocket for his mother's best underwear!

*Growing up near Elstree Studios meant that young Simon met many Hollywood film stars.*

As a young boy Simon enjoyed watching Hollywood stars laughing and joking at the parties his parents and their friends held. This experience gave him the confidence to mix with influential people and, as a result, Simon always had a feeling that he would end up working in the entertainment business.

In the 1960s, Elstree was a glamorous place to live, as it was home to the famous Elstree Studios. The Cowells' next door neighbour was a film producer who would entertain many legendary Hollywood stars, such as Elizabeth Taylor and Roger Moore. The Cowell family loved to mix in celebrity circles and Simon remembers feeling a thrill at the glamorous parties they held. "They were larger-than-life, attractive and happy. I thought: this is very glamorous. I'd love to live in a house like that and have a party like that."

*Remaining close to his family, Simon attends the final of* American Idol *with his brother, Tony.*

# Simon's school days

By the time Simon started school he had developed opinions on all sorts of things – and music was just one of them. He didn't enjoy school and couldn't see how physics and history were going to be useful to him in later life. In a music class, in which young Simon was asked to play the triangle, he raised his hand and said, "Miss, this is absolutely dreadful. Why are you making us do it?" Little did he know that it was this kind of bold, outspoken remark that would one day make him famous.

**HONOURS BOARD**

**Musicians that influenced Simon as a teenager:**

The Beatles

Elvis Presley

Bob Dylan

The Beach Boys

Frank Sinatra

*Dover College, the boarding school at which Simon spent several rebellious years.*

# INSPIRATION

The Beatles' rock-and-roll lifestyle had a strong influence on Simon while he was growing up. They were the first band to be seen living it up as celebrities: riding around in limousines, drinking champagne and holding wild parties. For the first time young people could look at this lifestyle and think "that could be me." Simon was one of those youngsters.

*Simon wished that he had been working in the music business in the 1960s so that he could have signed up the Beatles.*

At home, Simon continued to be **strong-willed**. He was so irritated by his parents' choice of music that he would often hide or even damage his mother's records so that she couldn't play them. He fought with his parents and would sometimes pack a bag and pretend to run away, creeping back hours later when he realised he had nowhere to go. He has said: "I think it's fair to say, I was the world's worst teenager."

When Simon was asked to leave his private school after only two months, his parents packed him off to Dover College, a boarding school on the south coast. He hated it and couldn't wait to get out. He ran small businesses to make some pocket money and left at the age of 16 with two O' levels (equivalent of GCSE today) to his name.

# starting at the bottom

Leaving school at 16, Simon had no idea of what he wanted to do with his life, except that he wanted to make some real money. After several unsuccessful interviews at a building site, at Tesco supermarket and for the Civil Service (in which he turned up to the interview in a pair of jeans), Simon finally landed a job as a **runner** at Elstree Studios.

Simon worked from 5 am until 7 pm and made £15 per week. But he didn't mind; he was in the entertainment industry and he had a hunch that he could make a lot of money there.

*Being a runner was a less-than-glamorous job, it involved running errands and making sure everything went smoothly.*

## TOP TIP

However high or low your position is in an organisation or company you should always treat everyone with good manners and respect.

elstreefilm&televisionstudios

Eric Cowell ran the property division at EMI Music Publishing so Simon's mother wrote to EMI to ask if there were any vacancies in the post room. The post room was a dark, damp and airless basement, but Simon was determined to move beyond it and onto better things. "From my first day on the job I began planning and scheming my way to the top of the business ... "

Several times a day Simon dodged the traffic pushing a heavy, wonky-wheeled trolley across four main roads. Knowing that his father was a director, several employees made

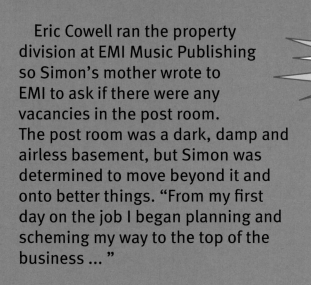

# INSPIRATION

Simon's parents instilled a **work ethic** in their son, by insisting that he earn his own pocket money. Even as a child Simon had a business head and knew how to make money! From the age of eight he would charge his neighbours £1 for cleaning their cars and, as he got older, he earned money as a babysitter, window cleaner and a carol singer.

nasty comments to Simon, but instead of them knocking his confidence, they just made him more determined to succeed.

*Simon is close to his mother and has even been called a 'mummy's boy'!*

# Budding entrepreneur

After a year working in the post room, Simon quit his job and started up his own record label – Fanfare Records. "I wanted to make records. Hit records. And I felt I had an instinctive understanding of what it took to make a hit record."

*Mike Stock, Matt Aitken and Pete Waterman (left to right), were a very successful song-writing team in the '80s and '90s. Simon thought of Pete as his **mentor** and described the day he met him as the most important in his career.*

Simon's first recording artist was a female singer from Seattle, USA, called Sinitta. He took a calculated business risk and spent £5,000 on producing her first hit single entitled *So Macho*. Simon's risk paid off. The single sold 900,000 copies, reached number 2 in the charts and made almost £1 million in profit. Simon was fast becoming a successful **entrepreneur**.

At this time, a song writing and producing team called Stock, Aitken and Waterman were becoming very popular.

*At the age of 16 Sinitta signed a record deal with Simon's record label, Fanfare Records. Simon and Sinitta are still close friends today.*

## HONOURS BOARD

### Simon's top pop stars of all time:

Robbie Williams — *He has the X factor. He's unpredictable and exciting to watch.*
Kylie Minogue — *She is great at re-inventing herself — just what is needed in today's pop world.*
Elton John — *He has an incredible song-writing talent, individuality and his music will be around forever.*

Simon asked Pete Waterman to write a song for Sinitta but he refused. Unwilling to take 'no' for an answer, Simon pestered Pete Waterman with daily phone calls, visits and meetings until he agreed to Simon's demands and wrote the hit record *Toy boy*. It sold millions of records for Sinitta and put Fanfare Records and Simon Cowell on the map.

# Wrestlers and Westlife

In the 1980s, BMG – one of the world's most successful music companies – was quietly tracking Simon Cowell's success. In 1989 BMG finally offered him a job as an **A&R** consultant. A&R stands for 'Artists and Repertoire' and involves looking for new talent. It was Simon's big break.

## WOW!

Simon passed up the chance to sign the Spice Girls. However, he did sign up Westlife!

*The success of Michael Jackson's* Thriller *music video made Simon realise that TV had the potential to sell music.*

Ahead of his time, Simon could see how powerful television was in selling music. In 1983 Michael Jackson's *Thriller* video had created the best selling record of all time. Television had a huge captive audience.

When the World Wrestling Federation (WWF) came to the UK, tickets for their show sold out Wembley Stadium in just 27 minutes. Simon figured that the wrestlers' popularity could probably also sell him a lot of records. He decided to make a music album with them and it sold 1.5 million copies.

## HONOURS BOARD

**Simon's early music acts:**
Breakfast show puppets Zig and Zag
Mighty Morphin' Power Rangers
TV actors, Robson and Jerome
Teletubbies
Five
Westlife

*Simon's huge boy band success story, Westlife present him with Celebrity of the Year award in 2004.*

# A day in the life of Simon Cowell

## TOP TIP

According to Simon, tenacity (sticking at something) is the maker of dreams, and if you want to succeed at something you need to persevere.

On the days when filming takes place for *American Idol*, Simon drives to the Hollywood studios in style in his Bugatti Veyron, one of the most expensive cars in the world.

He arrives on set and heads to his trailer, which has been specially adapted to have all the comforts of home such as a bedroom and a shower. Simon's fridge is stocked with his favourite lemon-lime mineral water, as well as with milk for his English breakfast tea.

He sometimes has a nap before the show, but about an hour before filming starts, Simon visits the set and has a chat with the producer. Just before he's due at the judges' table, Simon takes a shower to wake himself up, then heads into hair and make-up to be styled for the coming show.

*Simon is passionate about cars. He owns a fleet of cars.*

*The chemistry between* The X Factor *judges is the key ingredient to the show's success.*

Although Simon's life today is a far cry from his days as a young music executive desperate to make his mark, he works hard and takes only one holiday a year, usually to Barbados at Christmas. He remarks, "I don't believe in a five-day week or an eight-hour day. I believe in 24/7."

His busy schedule is crammed with filming TV shows or conducting auditions in the UK and the USA, as well as meetings, appointments, talk shows, interviews and music industry awards. He never misses a day's work or a day's filming.

Simon spends a lot of time flying – though these days it is by private jet. For example, while the live shows for *The X Factor* are taking place in UK, the auditions for *American Idol* are usually being filmed in the States, so Simon spends a lot of time in the air, crossing the Atlantic twice a week.

## HONOURS BOARD

**Simon Cowell's guide to success in auditions:**

Don't copy other performers. Be original.

Don't sing and dance at the same time. You'll run out of breath!

Make eye contact when you are performing. This is a sign of confidence.

Choose the right song or act for your personality and 'style'. Don't dress like a rock chick and then sing opera!

Eat and drink before an audition to keep your energy levels up.

Rehearse, rehearse, rehearse!

# Pop Idol mania

It's the mid-1990s. Simon Cowell and Pete Waterman are in a meeting with TV producers, screaming at each other at the tops of their voices. One of the producers listens in stunned silence and then says "If you two ever decide to do a TV show together, call me." Simon stops in mid-flow. The comment sticks in his mind.

*The original* Pop Idol *judge's line-up featured Simon, Pete Waterman, Nicki Chapman and Neil 'Dr' Fox (from left to right).*

## INSPIRATION

Simon hired Max Clifford to manage his public image. He regards this as one of the best decisions of his career. Max has kept 'bad' stories out of the newspapers and made sure 'good' ones go in!

In 2001, Simon Fuller, the former Spice Girls' manager approached Simon Cowell with the idea of producing a show called *Pop Idol*. Open to people aged 16 to 26, the lucky winner would receive a £1 million recording contract. Viewer participation was a major hook for the show enabling people to vote for their favourite performers by telephone, website, text or through the 'red button' on digital TVs.

*Pop Idol* went on air and was a massive hit with ratings as high as 10 million viewers. The build up to the live final of *Pop Idol 1* was compared to a political campaign as the country was divided in backing either Will Young or Gareth Gates to be crowned Pop Idol. The live final was held on 9 February 2002 and Will Young narrowly defeated the favourite, Gareth Gates. Will's **debut** single *Evergreen* sold 1.1 million copies in the first week. A second series of *Pop Idol* followed in 2003, and though this series lacked some of the excitement of series 1, Michelle McManus emerged as winner with Mark Rhodes as the runner-up.

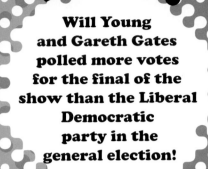

**Will Young and Gareth Gates polled more votes for the final of the show than the Liberal Democratic party in the general election!**

*Will Young and Gareth Gates went head-to-head in the first* Pop Idol *final in 2002. The battle was tense!*

# Breaking America

America wasn't instantly captured by the idea of a *Pop Idol* show. But US TV executives soon realised that a well-spoken British guy delivering brutal put-downs in America was going to be a massive hit. And they were right.

## TOP TIP

Simon believes that first impressions count. But this has been misinterpreted by many hopeful stars who have turned up to auditions dressed as lizards, wizards, vegetables, Star Trek characters and even Christmas trees complete with fairy lights!

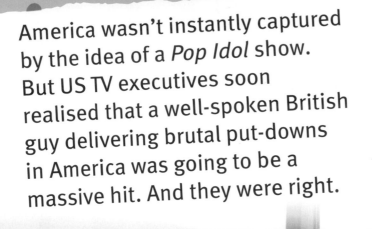

*Ex-Spice Girl Victoria Beckham guest judges on the* American Idol *panel in 2009 after Paula Abdul's surprise departure.*

*American Idol* was launched in 2002 and Simon's first insult on US television, to a young hopeful in Los Angeles was a rude **awakening** for America: "Not only do you look terrible, but you sound terrible. You're never going to be a pop star in a million years."

Simon was joined by judges Paula Abdul and Randy Jackson and the battles between them, on- and off- screen, added to the show's success. Almost overnight the judges were all over the news, magazine covers and prime-time talk shows. A glitzier affair than *Pop Idol*, *American Idol* is pure Hollywood glamour. The finals are staged at Hollywood's Kodak Theatre, excited crowds line the streets, searchlights scan the air and a plush red carpet is laid out for guests.

Since *Pop Idol* Simon has launched *American Inventor* and *America's Got Talent*. From his early days as an A&R man, through talent-show judge, Simon Cowell has emerged as a true TV genius. Simon's US success has led to him playing a **cameo role** in the box-office hit *Scary Movie 3*, as well as voice-overs for his character in *Shrek 2* and *The Simpsons*. Simon has also been asked to sing the US national anthem at baseball games – though apparently he cannot sing a word!

# WOW!

The popularity of American Idol has swept America like wildfire. The live finals attract almost 40 million viewers across the country and Mr Cowell himself is now the highest-paid presenter on US TV!

American Idol *presenter Ryan Seacrest (centre, kneeling) is presented with a star on Hollywood's Walk of Fame. Paula Abdul is on the left and Randy Jackson is on the right.*

# The X Factor

The x factor is that **elusive** quality. It is that certain something that sets you apart from the rest and draws people to you. Simon had been looking for the x factor in bands and singers for years. And ironically it was this phrase that was to make him super-famous.

## WOW!

Since her win in 2008 Alexandra Burke has signed a $3 million, five-album deal with Epic Records.

*Cheryl Cole (next to Simon) has proved to be a popular judge on* The X Factor.

Fresh from his American success, in 2004 Simon formed a company, Syco, and began work on a show called *The X Factor*. Simon knew if he could find contestants with this special quality, Syco Music and Syco TV could make millions.

In the summer of that year, 50,000 hopefuls turned up to auditions in cities all over the UK. A new set of high-profile judges provided some added excitement, with his producer friend Louis Walsh and the outspoken Sharon Osbourne, wife of rock legend, Ozzy, joining him on the panel. Dannii Minogue joined the show in 2007, and when Sharon walked out in 2008, pop icon Cheryl Cole (of pop band Girls Aloud) took her place.

Though Simon's cruel-to-be-kind approach continued, many performers were also lucky enough to see another side to him, with one finalist remarking: "Simon is one of the most charming and charismatic people I've ever met ... I consider myself very lucky to have

*Alexandra Burke returned to the stage of* The X Factor *in 2009 to sing her number 1 single,* Bad Boys.

been able to work with him." Leona Lewis and Alexandra Burke – both *X Factor* success stories – have achieved superstar status in the UK and US and are a testament to Mr Cowell's eye for a winner.

A master stroke of Cowell genius made *The X Factor* the extraordinary success story it is today. A compelling TV show – with viewing figures reaching 14 million – the UK audience are gripped.

## HONOURS BOARD

*The X Factor* **winners:**

Joe McElderry 2009

Alexandra Burke 2008

Leon Jackson 2007

Leona Lewis 2006

Shayne Ward 2005

Steve Brookstein 2004

# Simon's got talent

Simon's first attempt to launch *Britain's Got Talent* in 2005 failed when host-to-be, Paul O'Grady, moved to Channel 4. So Simon decided to launch it in America instead.

*The* Britain's Got Talent *team include former tabloid editor, Piers Morgan and TV actress, Amanda Holden.*

Simon instructed British TV presenter and panellist Piers Morgan on the US show *America's Got Talent* to "give it everything you've got to get the ratings up." He needn't have worried. It was another runaway TV success and the *Got Talent* **franchise** sold into 40 countries around the world bringing Simon's personal fortune to an estimated £200 million.

In 2007 when *Britain's Got Talent* finally launched in the UK, Simon invited his old favourites from *Pop Idol*, Ant and Dec to present the show. Piers Morgan and TV actress Amanda Holden joined him on the panel and open auditions were held across the UK. Britain's **eccentrics** and

*After becoming an Internet sensation, Susan Boyle found herself in the spotlight of the world's media.*

wannabes turned out in their droves to sing, dance and perform magic tricks – among many other oddball skills.

During series 3 of *Britain's Got Talent* a slightly scruffy-looking middle-aged lady appeared on the stage. There was laughter from some members of the audience. She sang *I Dreamed a Dream* from the show *Les Misérables*. The audience and the panel listened in jaw-dropping amazement at her incredible voice, but what happened next was even more astonishing. A video of Susan's performance was loaded onto YouTube and within a week 85 million people had viewed her performance. She was fast becoming an Internet superstar all over the world, proving that Simon Cowell's talent shows were far-reaching and could really rock the globe.

# WOW!

Though he dines at the finest restaurants in the world, Simon doesn't like to eat gourmet food. He prefers a traditional English breakfast, or simple food like rice pudding or baked beans. At his extravagant 50th birthday party in October 2009, guests sat down to a meal to celebrate – they were offered a choice of fish fingers and chips or shepherd's pie.

# From Mr Nasty to TV's hero

Not long after the launch of *Pop Idol* in 2001, Simon Cowell was voted one of the all-time Top 100 Worst Britons. He became a household name as TV's Mr Nasty. But his public image did start to shift, and we learned that Simon has a softer, more generous side.

## HONOURS BOARD

**Charities Simon supports:**
ARK (Absolute Return for Kids)
America Gives Back
Help for Heroes
PETA (People for the Ethical Treatment of Animals)

Simon gives a speech at the Battersea Dogs & Cats Home Collar and Cuffs Ball (2009).

...s & Cats Home **is a charity supporters through fundr**... ...enerosity of its

## WOW!

Simon Cowell produced a star-studded single to raise money for the victims of the Haiti earthquake in January 2010. The single was a cover of REM's song 'Everybody Hurts.' The artists involved in this project included, Susan Boyle, Leona Lewis and Rod Stewart. Simon had only ten days to put the single together!

In 2005 he appeared in two advertisements for the animal charity PETA, including an anti-fur campaign in which he was seen cuddling a dog. Several episodes of *American Idol* (called *Idol Gives Back*) have been devoted to raising money for disadvantaged children in Africa.

While he was a guest on the US show *Oprah* in 2008, Simon's generosity was revealed in front of millions of viewers. Having heard of the problems faced by a couple struggling to pay for their daughter's cancer treatment, Simon announced: "As of this afternoon, your mortgage has been paid off. But it doesn't stop there. If there are any more problems, I'm her guardian angel now."

Although Simon Cowell is sometimes boo-ed by *The X Factor* audience, he is seen more as a pantomime villain than a true one.

*Simon dances in a tutu with Sir Elton John for a charity performance of* Billy Elliot *in aid of children's charity The Place2Be, 2006.*

# The impact of Simon Cowell

On 1 July 2007 the Concert for Diana was held at the Wembley Stadium. It was organised by Princes William and Harry in memory of their mother who had died ten years earlier. Simon Cowell came on stage to applause from the audience of 90,000. "You've put on one heck of a show," he announced to the Princes from the stage. "In years to come, if you ever get tired of running the country, you can come and work for me producing TV shows." Prince William was stunned and delighted to receive such praise. The British public had taken Simon Cowell into their hearts.

*Simon's Beverly Hills office looks over Los Angeles and is a reminder that America is at his fingertips!*

Simon Cowell has led the way in music reality TV and has created shows in the style of soap operas and ensured the stars are always in the press. This is another stroke of Cowell genius. Who's on or off the panel? Which judge will weep, shout or walk off? One of the main features of Cowell's brand of music reality TV is to maintain the public's interest.

His impact is huge. Shows like *Strictly Come Dancing* in which the judges argue

*Top Shop owner, Philip Green and supermodel, Kate Moss, are rumoured to be involved in Simon's next project.*

and make rude remarks to each other and to the contestants – are all part of 'the Cowell effect'.

In the UK today, and even perhaps in the USA, Simon Cowell is one of the most influential men in music and television. His impact is such that it has even reached the ears of politicians. He has dined at 10 Downing Street with David Cameron and Gordon Brown. When Barack Obama gave Simon a name-check on the popular American *Tonight Show with Jay Leno*, it confirmed not only Mr Cowell's superstar status in the USA, but that 'the Cowell effect' had truly gone global.

# Have you got what it takes to be a music mogul? Try this!

1) How often do you listen to music?
a) Not very often. Just when the radio is on.
b) Most days I'll listen to music.
c) Sorry, let me just take my earphones out... What did you say?

2) What types of music do you listen to?
a) I only like rock. I can't stand other types of music.
b) I listen to anything that happens to be on the radio.
c) Well, my iPod is full. I have 74 albums on it – a mixture of R&B, soul, rap, rock, folk and pop.

3) Do you like pop?
a) No way. Pop is uncool and too commercial for me.
b) It's OK. I don't have any strong feelings about it.
c) Yes, I love pop. It's what most people want to listen to, isn't it?

4) Would you like a job that involves a lot of travelling?
a) No, I find travelling exhausting.
b) I wouldn't mind taking the train to London once in a while.
c) Wow, that sounds exciting and glamorous; yes please!

5) How do you react when people are critical of you?
a) I go mad! I don't like it when people criticise me.
b) I try to defend myself but I'm not very happy about it.
c) It rarely bothers me. I'm pretty confident in myself and my abilities.

6) Are you happy to offer your opinions on music and performing to others?
a) No, because I believe anyone can become a pop star if they practise hard enough.
b) Yes, but I don't have really strong opinions on music.
c) Absolutely! If I believe someone is good I'll say. If they are bad, well, I'll let them know that, too.

## RESULTS

Mostly As: Sorry to say this, but your future as a music mogul is in severe doubt! You do not have the musical interest or the commitment to succeed in this tough market.

Mostly Bs: You have an interest in music, but you probably need to work on your confidence and drive to ensure success in the music industry.

Mostly Cs: It sounds like you have what it takes to be a music mogul! Keep listening to music, work hard, stay focused and who knows?

# Glossary

**antidote**  An antidote takes away or balances out something unpleasant.

**awakening**  Just beginning or growing.

**A&R**  Stands for 'Artists and Repertoire'. An A&R executive is responsible for tracking down talented musicians and signing them to a record label in the hope that they will produce hits.

**cameo role**  When someone famous makes a brief appearance in a film or TV sitcom.

**deadpan**  Spoken deliberately showing no expression or emotion.

**debut**  Someone's first appearance in a role.

**eccentric**  Someone who is unconventional and sometimes peculiar.

**elusive**  Difficult to find or catch.

**entrepreneur** Someone who sets up and finances new business enterprises to make a profit.

**franchise**  A license sold by a company that allows a different person to sell goods or offer a service.

**infamous**  Being well-known for a bad quality or act.

**mentor**  An experienced person who trains or advises others.

**mogul**  An important or powerful person.

**music executive** A manager who works for a record label.

**runner**  A messenger and a general assistant in the film or TV industry.

**strong-willed**  Determined and independent.

**work ethic**  Having a belief in the value of hard work.

# Index

# INSPIRATIONAL LIVES

## Contents of titles in series:

### Barack Obama
978 0 7502 6089 3

Inauguration
Barack's family
Life in Indonesia
School and college
The world of work
Law school success
A day in the life of Barack Obama
Lawyer, husband, teacher and writer
The political life
Senator Obama
Winning the democratic nomination
The 2008 presidential election
The impact of Barack Obama
Have you got what it takes to be a politician?

### Jamie Oliver
978 0 7502 6268 2

Cooking up a storm
The young tearaway
Tinkering in the kitchen
London calling
The big break
The Naked Chef
A day in the life of Jamie Oliver
Oliver's Twist
Charity begins in the kitchen
Food fights
Jamie conquers America
A quiet celebrity
The impact of Jamie Oliver
Have you got what it takes to be a top chef?

### J.K. Rowling
978 0 7502 6273 6

A flash of inspiration
An imaginative child
Town and countryside in Tutshill
Teenage years
A secretary's story
Life in Portugal
A day in the life of J.K.Rowling

Difficult times
Harry Potter and the Philosopher's Stone
Catapulted
to fame
Harry on the big screen
A quiet celebrity
The impact of J.K.Rowling
Have you got what it takes to be a fiction writer?

### Lance Armstrong
978 0 7502 6269 9

The yellow jersey
Growing up in Texas
IronKid!
Cycling versus school
Turning professional
The tragic Tour
A day in the life of Lance Armstrong
Cancer
Treatment and recovery
The comeback
Turning point
Record breaker
The impact of Lance Armstrong
Have you got what it takes to be an endurance athlete?

### Richard Branson
978 0 7502 6271 2

The daredevil business man
Childhood challenges
School days
The accidental entrepreneur
Virgin in born
Recording in the countryside
A day in the life of Richard Branson
Virgin takes to the skies
The publicity machine
Mind the gap!
Changing the world
The final frontier
The impact of Richard Branson
Have you got what it takes to be an entrepreneur?

### Simon Cowell
978 0 7502 6272 9

The birth of TV's Mr Nasty
The early days
Simon's school days
Starting at the bottom
Budding entrepreneur
Wrestlers and Westlife
A day in the life of Simon Cowell
Pop Idol Mania
Breaking America
The X Factor
Simon's got talent
From Mr Nasty to TV's hero
The impact of Simon Cowell
Have you got what it takes to be a music mogul?

### The Beckhams
978 0 7502 6270 5

Together forever, eternally
Meet the families
Childhood
High kicks and kick offs
Spice up your life
Posh and Becks
A day in the life of the Beckhams
The football legend
Making the right moves
All for a good cause
California dreaming
Fashion, footy and beyond
The impact of the Beckhams
Have you got what it takes to be like the Beckhams?

WAYLAND